Introduction

My hope and pray[...] will learn what Je[...] [...] the Greatest Commandment is to Love God with all we are and to Love others as ourselves". From this study the Ministry of Love Him Love Them was born. It is my desire to create material that will help those who study it to become more like Jesus and learn to love those around us like never before.

This study comes from my personal journey of learning that God loves me, He wants me to love Him, and if I love Him I will love those around me. If I love those around me like He said I will never sin against Him or them.

I hope as you study this for the next six weeks you will see a life change for you as I did for me.

In Him,
David

How to use this Study:

You will find five days of study that will cover six weeks. On day six of each week you will review your notes from each day. On day seven of each week you should review and write a summary of what you learned during this week.

There is a tendency for some to try and run through the whole study in a few days but I want to caution you not to do this. I recommend you follow the outline here and meditate on what you are learning. There are many scriptures you will need to read and some you will need to read several times so please don't rush through.

Contents:

WEEK 1

Agape Love: The Bible teaches this love is an ACTION, not a FEELING.

The question we must answer is ... DO I LOVE LIKE THE LORD ASKS ME TO LOVE?

We will discover what the Bible teaches us about LOVE.

Most of us know there is a chapter in the Bible referred to as the LOVE chapter: 1 Corinthians 13. This chapter will be a large part of our study and will help make us aware of the meaning of God's LOVE. However, we will need to look at other parts of scripture as well to help us understand how God expects us to love.

DAY 1

To know and understand the Fathers LOVE, we must first know the Father. Read Romans 5:8 and Jerimiah 31:3.

Holiday Inn Express has many television commercials portraying people who stay in their hotels and wake up with newfound abilities that in reality require extensive study, education, experience, and hard work. In one such commercial a man passing through a nuclear reactor plant with a tour group slips in with all the engineers and gives the exact instructions needed to stop a nuclear reactor from blowing up. Once the mission is complete the head engineer goes to congratulate the man who gave the perfect instructions and introduce himself as he does not recognize him. He then learns he is NOT an Engineer nor is he even part of the team but in fact is just part of the tour group passing through. The man completes his introduction by saying "I don't work here, but I did stay at a Holiday Inn Express last night".

As funny as this commercial sounds... that is not the way it works in real life. For this man to have performed such a task he would have needed: previous diligent study, knowledge of the reactor, and understanding of the reactors functions. We don't just wake up one day with the ability to understand the instructions required to perform Agape Love either. For us to know how to perform the actions of Agape Love we need to diligently study God's word, know Him, and understand Him. Read Romans 12:1-2.

To LOVE like the Father we must KNOW the Father. We only have His power, strength, and peace if we KNOW Him. John 10:10 says that ONLY Jesus makes life full. Only a relationship with Jesus gets us to the Father Ephesians 1:3-10.

Read John 3:16, I realize many of you know this verse from memory. BUT, I want you to take the time to read the verse as if it is the very first time and focus on what God did to show his LOVE for YOU.

Now, read John 8:18-19 and 27-29.
What did God do to show His LOVE for us?

_____

What did Jesus say we must do to see the Father?

_____

God sent His only son to be our sacrifice for sin. This is an unbelievable and incredible act of LOVE. God cared enough about you and me that He _gave_ His only son, Jesus. Jesus then tells us, "If you do not KNOW me and LIFT me up, then you will not know the Father." Jesus showed the same LOVE to us when He went to the cross to die for you and me.

Do you know Him?
Do you lift Him up as your Savior?

Is He THE LORD of your life and the basis on which you make every decision?

Before we can attempt to understand God's Love we must first KNOW Him.

If you do not KNOW God; If you have not asked Him to be THE LORD of your Life; If you have not surrendered all your wants and desires for His, please know you can take this opportunity to pray with me now and do so.

Dear God,
I want to KNOW you. I want to understand your LOVE. I finally realize I can only do this by lifting up your Son Jesus. I want Jesus to be my Lord and Savior. Please forgive me of my sins and make me one with you. Jesus, please fill me with your LOVE and make me a member of your family. Take control of my life today. Amen.

If you just prayed this prayer, I want to be the first to welcome you to the Family of God.

If you have already asked Jesus to live in your heart, I want to challenge you to take a moment and ask God to allow His Holy Spirit to work IN you and THROUGH you so this Bible study will allow you to become a REAL LOVER of God, your spouse, your children and the people God has placed in your life.

Are you ready to make a change?

Notes:

LOVE IN ACTION

As we learned yesterday, God showed us that LOVE requires ACTION.

God had to SEND His Son. If God had just sat in Heaven and said "Well, I love these people, I really do have feelings for them, but I am not going to do anything for them to provide a way for them to be redeemed." If that were the case we could simply say, LOVE is a feeling. However, God made it very clear by setting the standard, LOVE requires something of us. We must ACT!

From the very beginning with Adam, God showed His love by doing something: an action.

       • He provided for Adam.

Read Gen 2:20-22. What did God provide for Adam to show him His Love?

_____

God loves His creation continually. God could have easily left Adam alone with the animals and the land. However, God decided to make Adam complete by providing him a helpmate. God showed His LOVE to Adam through His action.

Read Exodus 3: 7-12

What did God see that His people needed?

_____

What did He DO?

_____

_____

What did He use?

_____

What was Gods promise to Adam?

_____

God saw the oppression of His people and decided to deliver them. God went into ACTION. He WENT to Moses and told him that he would be the one to deliver His children.

When Moses responded "But, God........" God said "I will GO with you." Never has God asked someone to do something that He wouldn't be a part of or Go with them to accomplish the task. He also equips us for EVERY thing He calls us to do, even LOVE the unlovable. God has never seen His children in distress and not come to help them. (Somebody just shut down with that statement. You are in distress and you feel like God is nowhere near you. I want you to know this, God is always near, Psalms 34:18-20, but sometimes we are allowed to walk through the fire to be made pure, 1 Peter 1:7)

God is ALWAYS present and willing to get involved and stay involved until the task is complete.

God has always provided. He provided for Adam and He will provide for us today. His Love abounds and He is always putting His Love into action. He provided eternal life for you and me by sending His Son.

Take a moment and List some ways God has provided for you and is providing for you.

_____

_____

_____

Pray and Thank God for His Love. Thank Him that He is showing His Love in your life by being actively involved with you.

Notes:

Gods Patience

Psalms 86:15
But you, Lord, are a compassionate and gracious God, slow to anger, abounding in love and faithfulness.

God's Love (AGAPE) is demonstrated with action. What we will learn in 1 Corinthians 13 is although Agape is a noun it is demonstrated by action. In the same manner, patience also requires action.

Read Psalms 103: 8-10

What do these verses say about God? What has God not done?

_____

Sometimes we see other people living a life that is totally out of line with God's word and we wonder why God is allowing them to prosper.

Read Jeremiah 7:23-25

Why do you think God continued to be patient with the children of Israel for years?

_____

God was faithful in His attempt to reach His children. He had prophet's there every day. They arose early to tell His message. God never sleeps and never waivers from His attempt to get us to turn from our wicked ways. Isn't that awesome that we have someone so patient AND faithful that LOVES us so much?

_____

_____

Now read 2 Peter 3:9

Why do you think God is patient?

_____ _____

God's desire is for us to return to Him. He wants to see
us standing on the streets of gold with Him and His Son
Jesus. We should thank Him daily for not giving us what
we deserve. We deserve death but through His LOVE for
us He has given us Christ.

Pray now to thank Him for not giving you what you
deserve and for being patient with you.

Remember: SIN is missing the mark.

Take some time right now to thank Him for not giving
you what you deserve for your actions today. Also take
this time to pray to God, Psalms 139:23-24

Notes:

NEVER FAILING

Jos 21:45
Not one of the LORD's promises to Israel failed. Every one of them was fulfilled.

Not too long ago I purchased a new battery for my truck. The truck is a heavy-duty work truck so I spent the big bucks to get the "Heavy-Duty, Never Fails" battery. Well as you might have guessed it failed. I took it back to the store and after all the questions and the test they determined the battery had failed. My super-duper, never fail, battery had let me down; it failed to provide for me as advertised.

Although batteries and people fail me, and I them, God never does. I have never had to file a claim against God for "failure to provide"!

He is ALWAYS there and, as we will see, He never fails.

Read Luke 1: 72-77

What does this show us about Gods faithfulness?

_____

God made a promise to Abraham and here many years later is the announcement of that promise. God promised salvation and He sent His Son to fulfill His promise.

Read Psalm 34: 17-22

What does it say The Lord hears?

_____

The Lord is close to whom?

_____

Who is going to be pardoned?

_____

Do you see it? We have a part here; we have to CALL on HIM, we need to be BROKEN, (not prideful... We will dive into this in the next section) and we must trust in HIM.

God promises His presence but if we are not trusting in Him or humbled before Him it is going to be difficult for us to see Him or hear Him. Also if we have _____ in our hearts He will not hear our prayers.

Read Psalms 66:18-19

Read Psalm 71

List all things you can see here about how God is constant.

_____

_____

_____

The Psalmist is showing us that God has been constant through his life. God delivered him and taught him from his childhood all the way through to his elder years. We can hold fast that God was concerned about us from before there was time (Ephesians 1:4) ....." And knit me together in my mother's womb" (Psalm 139:13)

We also see in this Psalm that God should be praised for never forgetting us, even when we suffer hardship....v20. He shows us that God also restores us to even greater honor than before if we just hold fast.....v21.

Pray and thank God for his never changing hand. If you feel like God has forsaken you then you need to talk to Him about that. God already knows your heart; however, He wants you to talk to HIM. Never forget, He is your Heavenly Father.

Notes:

DAY 5

REJOICE NOT IN INIQUITY

One of the last things we need to see about our God is He is disgusted with sin. You may ask why this is important. God disciplines us and the following explains why.

Some may say, "Well, God allows sin to happen so He must not be worried about it". The explanation for this is that God has given us Free Choice; we have the choice to live a righteous life or a sin-filled life. Be assured it does grieve His heart and He will chasten His own for it. Those that won't turn from it hurt Him.

SIN causes SEPARATION.
SIN causes PUNISHMENT.

Repented Sin leads to FORGIVENESS.
Repented Sin leads to ONENESS

Read Isaiah 59: 1-2

What does this say about sin and God?

_____

_____

This makes it very clear that if we have NEVER repented of our sins and asked Jesus into our hearts God will not look toward you. If we have come to a point of salvation in our lives God still holds un-repented sin against us as far as our Fellowship with Him is concerned. He will not forsake us because of the sin but He will not fellowship with us until we repent. If we have sin in our lives God is not going to answer our prayer. God is a righteous and Holy God and cannot look on sin.

Maybe the Holy Spirit has brought something or multiple things to your heart that you need to ask God to forgive you for right now. If so, take this opportunity to repent.

Lamentations 3:40
Let us examine our ways and test them, and let us return to the LORD.

God wants to commune with us but we must be willing to be honest with Him about our heart.

1 John 1:9
If we confess our sins, He is faithful and just and will forgive us our sins and purify us from all unrighteousness.

Notes:

God and me

OK! This is where we decide if we want to live a life filled with LOVE, JOY, and HAPPINESS?

Now that we understand God has GIVEN us His Son so that we might be at one with Him. We have seen He provides for us. We also have seen His patience, His faithfulness, and His disgust of sin. We must grasp these truths about God to have a solid foundation, to experience his LOVE (agape) and to show this kind of love.

Now we come to the most critical part of our lesson thus far. We must understand that God never stops LOVING us no matter what, but do we Love Him? This is the cornerstone for LOVING others. If we can't LOVE God then how can we truly LOVE others?

So let's look at how we are to LOVE Him and begin to live it over the next few weeks and for the rest of our lives.

If you LOVE me...

Let's start today by discovering what God wants us to do to show our LOVE for Him.

Read John 14:21-24

What does Jesus say about the words He is speaking?

_____

You must grasp this.....Jesus is not speaking His words but the words of the Father. We must realize, to show our Love for God we must do what? (Read John 14:21-24 again)
If we have His commands and keep them, then it is he who loves Him and if we love Him, we love the Father. There is a key point we must look at here. If you look at this closely, we can't LOVE one without the other. Jesus said, "YOU love Me then the Father loves you". This all goes back to our discussion in week 1 about why we must receive Christ as our Savior.

NOW ONE QUESTION APPEARS, How do we love Jesus?

Read John 14:21 again

We must keep His commands. Now we have to discover what His commands are. Are they the 10 commandments? Or is there something else?

Read Matthew 5:17

What does Jesus say about the law?

He didn't come to destroy it or change it, He came to fulfill it. As we continue tomorrow, we will look at HOW Jesus came to fulfill the Law.

Pray now and thank God for His law and for sending His Son to redeem us and to teach us how we should live. Thank Him for helping us to understand HOW to love Him.

Notes:

When we look at the Law we will also look at what Jesus said about it. Remember the Law Jesus was referring to was the Mosaic Law. Today most of us think about the law as the 10 commandments. This is not what Jesus was referring to but I do think we need to cover them here because they are a measuring rod for our lives. We will discuss later the way Jesus summed up the whole Law and what we do with that.

COMMANDMENTS

Read Exodus 20

What did God say about other gods?

_____

This means we are not to have anything in our lives that is more important than He is. We can worship money, family, cars, houses, and many other things.

So again, to LOVE (agape) God we must not have anything more important to us than Him.

What does Exodus 20 say about how we are to speak of God?

_____

We should never take God's name in vain. This not only includes the most obvious which is using Gods name to curse but in any way that we bring the name of The Lord down.

For us to LOVE God we must first realize that He is Holy and we must always keep Him above everything else. God should be personal to us and easy to talk with. However, we should never think of God as just another "good ole' boy" or "the man upstairs", God is much more than that.

Read the following:
Exodus 20:26
Psalms 11:7
Psalms 22:3
Matthew 5:48
Luke 18:19
John 7:28
Romans 1:22-23
1Peter 1:15-16

List below all the things you learned about God and His character:

_____

_____

_____

_____

_____

As you can see, God is definitely not just another "good ole boy". He is HOLY, JUST, RIGHTEOUS, TRUE, and EVERLASTING. In order to love someone it is important that we know who he or she is. This is also imperative in knowing how to love God. I hope through the above scriptures that you have been able to develop a true picture of He is a friend who sticks closer than a brother does, but He is God. He sent His Son to die for us. He has claimed us for His own if only we are willing to accept Him. And He is above all others. He is the Alpha and Omega, the first and the last, the beginning, and the end. Read Rev 22:13

Remember His Day
Read Exodus 20:8

We won't spend a lot of time here; however, I want us to
see how this command can communicate LOVE. Can you
think of a way or ways to show your love for God
through this commandment?

I would say respect. Respecting Him on this day for the
wonderful creation He has given us. This is where we
need to say how do you keep the Sabbath Holy? I think
one of the most important ways is to spend it with Him. I
believe we should try at all costs to spend it with other
believers. Read 1 Thessalonians 5:11

What are the effects of gathering with other believers?

_____

We see that we can comfort one another and edify (lift
up) one another. We need to realize that life here on
earth is difficult and we need each other to lean on and
learn from. We can't do life alone!
If your attitude about the Sabbath day is not in keeping
with Gods law to keep it Holy, pray now and ask God to
change your attitude.

Psalms 42: 1-5

WHAT do you see here about the Sabbath (Holy Day)?

_____

David said I went with the multitude. Why do you think
this was important?

_____

I think David knew where two or more gathered God would also be in the midst of them. I think David knew in his times of trouble he needed to worship with others. He needed to encourage them and be encouraged by them.

Take time to pray now and thank God that He has provided a place for you to worship with other believers. If you have been lazy or just had an attitude of "I don't want to go to His house to keep the Sabbath Day Holy, ask God to forgive you. Commit to Him now that you are ready to change.

Notes:

DAY 4

I HAVE TO HONOR WHO?

Read Exodus 20:12

Who are we supposed to honor?

_____

What happens when we do?

_____

This is the only commandment of these 10 given to Moses that comes with a promise.

We need to look at what it means to HONOR. Why honor them? When to honor them? Remember what we are studying here. We are studying about LOVE and how to "do" it.

In the Hebrew language the word for honor is a verb....action.

HONOR: to respect, take advice from (as long as it is not unlawful or ungodly), to praise, and to take care of. (Matthew 15:4-6)

Read Psalm 139:13

What does this say about God, parents and you?

_____

God knew who your parents were going to be before the foundation of the earth was made. He knew you even while you were still in your mother's womb. If we believe God is all-knowing, He is sovereign, and nothing surprises Him, then we must believe God chose our parents.

Some of you may be asking "what if I have parents that abused me or left me or have not come to know Christ"? What then? What now?

To you who have been abused, left and disowned; God does not condone any of these behaviors. However, God does not want us to talk badly about our parents nor should we seek revenge. I have a friend, Cheryl, who I watched live this principle out in her life. I have asked her to share a little about her story.

I grew up in a home where my father was an alcoholic. When he drank he became abusive. He abused me, my sister, and my mother. My mother was an angry domineering, difficult, and demanding woman. Neither of my parents knew Christ when I was growing up, yet God in his kindness, saved me at age 16. God commands in Ephesians 6:1-3 to honor our parents. One of the Ten Commandments in Exodus 20:12 is to honor your parents. The word honor means to show reverence and place value upon. God is not telling us to honor our parents when they merit it, but He tells us this because of the position He has put them in. God is sovereign over the era of time I was born into, the country I was born in, and the family and parents He chose for me. There is purpose in everything God commands, and that includes honoring ungodly parents.

God used my parents to show me the depths of my own sinful, selfish heart. This exposing of my heart left me with a choice: to ignore this or be changed by God. God allowed me to be salt and light, pushing back the darkness in my parent's lives. It is a dichotomy for sure; God changing me, and God using me to change them. My father was an unbeliever until the last 5 years of his life, when He did come to know Christ as savior. I need to never give up hope for my parents. Always continue displaying and speaking the love of the gospel to your unsaved parents. Recently my mother was diagnosed with dementia. I have moved across several states to be near her. It has been a sacrifice and she is difficult, demanding, and unappreciative. Why am I caring for her? Because God has commanded that I revere her, and place value in her. At this time in her life she cannot care for herself well. Ultimately the life of a believer is to bring glory to God and be changed into the image of Christ. My life does not belong to me, but has been purchased by Christ's blood for His purposes. Caring for my mom is one of those purposes.

Jesus submitted himself to his earthly parents and his heavenly Father. At some point we are no longer directly under our parent's authority, but we never grow out of the command to honor them. While my parents may not have changed for most of their lives, God has continued to change my heart, attitudes, responses, and actions to be more like Christ. Honoring your parents by showing unmerited love, favor, kindness, and placing value in them is a sure way to bring Glory to God and to bear eternal fruit. "Children, obey your parents in everything, for this pleases the Lord". Col. 3:20

Cheryl's story very clearly explains WHY we are to honor those God commands us to honor.

How difficult it is for us to honor God, whom in this life we can't tangibly place our arms around, if we are not even able to honor those we can see and touch now. God chose your parents and we need to honor His choice. Remember, God entrusted His one and only Son to earthly parents.

WHEN:
God did not place a time limit in His word providing an end to when we would no longer need to honor our parents. This is a forever command, even though your parents may have left this earth. We must continue to always give our parents respect. This is true also when we are discussing our parents with other people.

Notes:

Kill......Certainly not me!

Read Exodus 20:13

Most of us can say that we have never taken anyone's life. Most of us can say that we have never even thought of such an act. But, if we think this commandment is only talking about killing, we are making a big mistake.

Read Psalm 25:18

What does this say about lying?

It is clear to me to lie about someone, or to gossip about a person in such a way that would damage their reputation is equivalent to taking a sword and killing them.

Read Matthew 5:21-22

Now let's compare ANGER and murder.

If we have anger in our heart towards our brother, Jesus said we are as guilty as if we had killed them. Anger and hatred toward someone else is nothing to laugh about...God doesn't. We can't leave this topic without discussing the issue of abortion.

Read Psalm 139:13

How do you think God feels about abortion based on this verse?

God makes it clear that He knew us even when we were in the womb. If this is the case then God recognizes life's beginning at the point of conception.

Read Deuteronomy 32:9

As hard as this may be to accept and understand. God is the giver of life and the one who takes life away. This makes it very clear that we have no say in the matter of life and death.

Allow me to take a moment to say to those of you who have had an abortion, there is forgiveness. God says that if we repent of our sins and turn from our wicked ways, He is faithful and just to forgive us. He is faithful to forgive ALL sin. Don't think God can't love you for the things you have done.

Let's take the rest of our time today and ask God to forgive us. If you have murdered someone in any way, ask God to forgive you and repent. If you have already asked for and been forgiven for such an act, thank God now for His grace and forgiveness.

If you are still experiencing guilt after having truly repented, this is not from God.
Read Psalm 103:12 and claim this promise from God.

Notes:

DAY 1

Don't look too long......

Read Exodus 20:14

This is very straightforward. We are not supposed to have sexual relations with anyone other than our spouse. If you are not married you may be saying, "Well, I don't have a spouse......so, I'm looking!" Hold on, my friend this still applies to you also.

Read Matthew 5:27-28

What does this say about adultery?

_____

Jesus is saying....If you even look at another person with sexual thoughts you have committed adultery. If this is the case then He is saying that sexual relations were designed only for marriage and that you should remain faithful in that relationship even with your eyes and your heart.

Read 1 Corinthians 7:2-3

Paul states very clearly that because of sexual sins we should have only one spouse and only show affection to them.
Let's spend some time here asking God to search our hearts and make known any sin, but especially any sexual sins. Let's ask for forgiveness, repent, and turn from those ways.

If you are in the middle of an affair or thinking about starting one, please go to someone (not the person your involved with) now and ask him or her for help in confronting this issue. Also, some of you need to get on the phone right now and break off a relationship and go to God and confess. You need to be honest with yourself here. Don't try in any way to justify this. If you are not married it is against Gods law and if you are married and you are involved with someone other than your spouse you are breaking these same laws. STOP THIS NOW!

Notes:

DAY 2

Give that back, it's not yours

Read Exodus 20:15

It again is clear we are not supposed to take something that is not ours. This commandment people seem to easily find ways to justify. We say things like, well he took this from me so I'm taking this from him or he owes me money so I'll just take this instead. It is stealing. If you didn't pay for it or if the person it belongs to didn't willingly give it to you, you stole it.

I have seen people receive too much change back when making a purchase and justify it as "oh well, their loss, they should have been paying attention". I have seen people walking out of stores and not paying for things because the cashier overlooked it....if they know it was a mistake and did not rectify it, it is stealing.

But let's go a little deeper here and talk about the IRS and God. How many of us have cheated the IRS? (Read Matthew 22:21)

This is very clear; if our government requires us to pay taxes, then as bad as it hurts we must pay them.

What does this verse also say about God?

_____

Read Leviticus 27:30
Numbers 18:26
Nehemiah 13:12
Malachi 3:10

What do these verses say about our tithe and God?

_____

Let me be real blunt here......

Tithing is not an issue that is up for debate. We must pay our tithes. God expects this for several reasons. This is the way the church pays its staff, reaches out to a lost world, and helps disciple believers. Another reason: if we can't trust God to provide in our finances we probably are not going to have enough faith to get through a sickness, job loss, or a problem in our marriage either. This is a matter of obedience. How can we say we Love God if we can't obey Him?

Notes:

DAY 3

Read Exodus 20:16

Remember when we talked about murder? We discussed how lying about someone could murder their reputation.

We need to be very careful when we are requesting prayer for people who are going through a struggle. It is not always, and very seldom, necessary to share details especially if the person you are talking about has not said is ok to share. You should also never say anything about someone you wouldn't say to his or her face, or to Gods. Loving another person sometimes requires you to keep your lips zipped.

Read Exodus 20:17

Covet? What does this mean?

Here is the definition found in the Nelson Bible Dictionary.

COVETOUSNESS....
An intense desire to possess something (or someone) that belongs to another person. The Ten Commandments prohibit this attitude Exodus 20:17 and Deuteronomy 5:21. Covetousness springs from a greedy self-centeredness and an arrogant disregard for Gods law. The Bible repeatedly warns against this sin. Joshua 7:21, Romans 7:7 and 2Peter 2:10 (from Nelson's Illustrative Bible Dictionary Copyright (C) 1986, Thomas Nelson Publishers)

If you look very closely here it is not saying a wish or a want to have something similar to someone else. If I saw a new car and said "Wow, I would like to have a car like that!" there is nothing wrong with the desire. It becomes a sin when I fix my heart on this car and it becomes the focal point of all I think about and want...that is coveting. Also, it means to have a desire so deep that you resent any person who has that car. You then resent God for not giving you the same thing someone else has.

Notes:

DAY 4

Read James 2: 8-11

What does this say about the law?

God gave us 10 Commandments so we all have the same measuring rod. Nowhere are we told, "If you keep 8 of the commandments you are better than someone who only keeps 2". We are told, if we break one, we break the whole law.

Let's not stop here though, when we understand what Christ said about the Law, then we begin to understand Love. Many churches and organizations have signs or plaques that state the TWELVE COMMANDMENTS. This can be confusing, because most of us are only familiar with the Ten Commandments.

Read Matthew 22: 36-38
What does this say about the law?

_____

The man in this story came to Christ hoping to justify himself. He was hoping that Christ would answer his question with one of the commands from the Law. He had not broken any of these. However, Christ's response of "Love the Lord your God with all your heart, all your soul and your entire mind" was perplexing.
What does this mean?

CHRIST said you can keep all the laws you want but if you don't love God, nothing else matters! Loving God is the First and greatest commandment. Does this abolish the Law? NO! It is the Law. Just in looking at the 10 Commandments we see that they are about Love, Love God and Love others. If we Love God we won't sin against Him. If we Love people we won't sin against them. It is the only way we can truly keep the 10 Commandments.

We have looked at several ways we can keep the 10 Commandments without truly loving God. We saw you can live without taking someone's life, without committing adultery, without stealing. But if we look at what Christ said, it takes Love not to lust, it takes Love not to gossip and lie about someone, and it takes Love to give unto God what is Gods. If you don't understand how to Love and you don't do what is required to Love, you also cannot keep His laws. (Love the Lord and Love others)

Notes:

With what?

Yesterday we learned that Christ said we must LOVE God with all our HEART, SOUL and MIND. What does this mean?

Let's look at the heart first.

Read Genesis 6:5, 17:7, and 27:41 Matthew 15:17-20

What do these verses say about the heart?

_____

_____

Look at the conversations in these versus that were not expressed aloud, the conversation was in the heart. God said the thoughts of his heart are evil. Abraham mocked God in his heart and had doubt. Esau had hate in his heart.

So we have doubt, hate and many emotions that can take place in the heart.

I think this is what God was saying when He said to LOVE me with all your heart? Are the attitudes of Abraham and Esau attitudes of love? Remember the commandments, don't steal, don't lie, and don't covet? I think He is looking for a heart of joy, forgiveness, unselfishness, and willingness. We must get rid of these other things and have what God is looking for in our heart to have a heart for Him and a true love for him. Deuteronomy 28: 47-48
Psalm 13:5, 19:8, 24:4-5, 28:7, 36:10, 45:1, 57:7

We could go on and on listing scriptures about joy, happiness and the peace we should have in our hearts. We can see here from this list of verses that God wants us to be joyful, upright, and steadfast. This is what it means to love Him with all your heart. If you take a glass and fill it to the brim and then drop in a piece of ice.....what happens? The water starts to come out. This is the picture we need to have of our hearts. If our hearts are consumed with God and the joy, peace and happiness He gives and if we have a forgiving heart, a heart willing to give, then there is no room for evil. WE will have a heart that is ALL Gods.

Notes:

There's more?

Read Matthew 22: 36-38

Yes, now we must love Him with all our soul

Read Genesis 2:7

This is referring to the difference between you and all other life forms. This part of us will live on after death. God is saying is "I must control your soul". When you are born you have control of your soul. But, what God is saying is, at some point you must give it to Him through accepting Christ. If you do not do this then you cannot truly love Him.

Our soul is referred to as the seat of our emotions. You can't truly say you love God if your emotions don't reflect it. Now, I'm not saying we can't have a bad day, or there aren't medical reasons that can cause your emotions to be out of whack. But, what I AM saying is if you find yourself always with emotions of anger, hate, unforgiveness, and resentment towards God and man, then I believe the scripture says you don't love God as He is asking you to.
Read Matthew 6:14
Ephesians 4:31-32
Matthew 5:22

These verses show us again the attitude and emotion God wants us to have. These are His commands.

DAY 2

ONE MORE THING! YOUR MIND.
Romans 7:25
Ephesians 4:17
1 Corinthians 2:16

What do you think Paul is saying about the mind?

I believe Paul is saying that we must have our minds on the things of God, then I can serve The Lord. He is saying that if I depend on the flesh I am going to fail. He says I need the mind of Christ. The mind is where everything begins. 2 Corinthians 10:5 tells us we must take every thought captive. If we fail to do this it leads to the heart and soul being sinful. First, we have the thought of sin, then the emotion (feeling) of sin and then ultimately the act of sin.

We must grasp this concept and take our minds back from Satan. We cannot live a righteous life without having our mind under control.

This is the first battlefield where we will face Satan. Fortunately, we've been given the armor to fight him.

Read Ephesians 6:11-17

What is the protection for the mind?

_____

The helmet of salvation, through our receiving of Christ, He has given us armor to fight against Satan and the attacks on our mind. But do beware; He did say to put-on the whole armor. We cannot expect to ask Jesus into our hearts and then Satan runs off and leaves us alone. He will attack us! So we must put on the whole armor of God.

DAY 3

Read Matthew 22:39-40
And now, we have the rest of the story.

Christ says we must love our neighbor as ourselves. What does this mean?
This is where we start to put things together. First some of us have to answer the question. How do I love myself? We love ourselves by not knowingly putting ourselves into danger, making sure we have food, clothing, a place to sleep and money. Point being, we take care of ourselves. We don't, out of desire, go sleep in the streets or play in them. We don't shed our warm clothes when it's cold. Most people value their lives and want to take care of themselves.

Please note here, this scripture has been misinterpreted to mean we must love ourselves before we can love others. God never commanded us to love ourselves. He in fact has told us; LOVE Him first and then others but never ourselves.

You wouldn't go around saying bad things about yourself, you wouldn't knowingly cheat yourself out of money, and you wouldn't want your spouse to have an affair on you. Let's look at this in scripture.

Read Romans 13:9-10
What does this say?

It is saying Love your neighbor and you will automatically keep the commandments. You won't do something against your neighbor, your spouse, your children, your parents, or anyone else if you truly Love them.

Take some time now to ask God to show you who you do not love this way and ask Him to give you the strength to change it.

DAY 4

Let's spend the last two days of this unit looking at other ways we need to show our love toward God.

Worship, what does it mean?

To give reverence to God who deserves it. Webster also says an "Intense Love for"

We should worship God for what He has done and because of His love for us. He gave us HIS son and has promised us eternal salvation if we accept Jesus. I think He also knew we would worship things and people and this is why the first three commandments deal with worship. Let's review them quickly...Read Exodus 20:1-7.........God starts by reminding us He is God. He is the ONLY God and He is the One who delivers. He then says we are to have no other gods before Him. He must be FIRST in our lives. Then, He said No idols, we must have faith for who He says He is and worship only Him. This means don't buy things or make things and let that be what you worship. It also means don't attach to things and worship them. He is God alone, we need nothing else. He then said, thou shalt not bow down to any of the things you made, bought, or were given. We should only bow to Him. Get it? This is worship, bowing to Him. Giving Him the reverence He deserves. Then God goes on to tell us about His name. His name is sacred and not to be used carelessly. We should give His name honor.

Read Psalm 29:2, 66:4 and 95:6
Can you say this is a picture of you?

Are there things in your life you are worshiping in place of God that He wants you to give up? Pray and ask Him to show you if there is something in your life that is taking His place.

Praise:

To lift up, glorify...usually in song.
Read Psalms 7:17 and 9:1-2

Is this a picture of you?
Are you happy about what God has done for you?
In the Psalms, David continually talks about how God has and is going to deliver him, and David says "I will praise you!" Are you praising God? Do you find it hard sometimes to praise God? If so, take some time to think about the things He has done. Start with His creation, His Son, and His love for you. His love for us should make us all praise Him.

Take some time now to just spend praising Him for what He has and is doing in your life. You may want to write some of them down. If you are having trouble thinking of the things He has done.....Ask Him to show you......you can start with the air you are breathing right now, and the fact that you can breathe. Next, what about the creation He is allowing you to witness.

Notes:

DAY 5

The last way to show God we Love Him.

My wife has taught in the Middle School Ministry at our church. When she begins to teach her kids about their relationship with God, one of the questions she asks is how many of them pray. Most often only a few of them will respond positively and of those who do, they admit it is only occasionally. She then asks how many of them have boyfriends (she only teaches girls), most all of them respond YES. The next question is: "how many times a day do you talk to your boyfriend". They all answer with at least once a day and most of them many, many times a day. I'm sure you can see where she is going with this. Her next question is..."what do you think your relationship with your boyfriend would be like if you only talked to Him as often as you talk to God"?

How can we say we love God and He is the most important thing to us if we never or rarely talk to Him? It's kind of difficult to have a relationship with anyone if we never communicate with him or her.

I don't know about you, but my wife wouldn't want to be around me very long if I never spoke to her, or if when I did it was only to ask her for something I wanted.

PRAYER, what is it?
For most of us it is asking, begging, or crying out to God for what we need. Usually this only happens when we are in need. Imagine if you only heard from your best friend when they wanted something from you. What if the only time your children spoke to you was when they wanted money or food (that may be closer to reality than we would like to admit). You wouldn't feel much love though, would you? God wants to communicate with us. This is the reason He created us...for fellowship. Fellowship requires more than a one sided conversation.

The Bible tells us to "pray without ceasing" in 1 Timothy 5:17..... Does this mean we should also "ask without ceasing"?

Matthew 6:8 says "Our Father knows what we need before we even ask." Does this mean we don't have to ask? No, it means that He loves us so much; He already knows what we need. How awesome is that?

Prayer is a method for us to communicate our needs, our thankfulness, and our praise to our Father. The Bible is how He communicates with us. If we are not sitting quietly, meditating, and listening we will never experience the full benefit of prayer. This is HUGE and I don't want you to miss it. We MUST meditate on His word and listen if we ever expect to know Gods plan for our lives. This is also how we are able to receive His direction for our lives

Read James 5:16
What does this tell us about prayer?

_____

Read Matthew 6:6-13
What do you learn?

_____

We learn He is Holy and His will is going to be done. He provides. He forgives. He gives guidance. He delivers us from evil. What a Father, what a friend!

Take a few moments now to just talk to God. Meditate on what you have just learned. Ask Him to forgive you for neglecting Him. Ask Him to allow His Holy Spirit to overwhelm you right now.

WEEK 5

DAY 1

Now we arrive at the tough part. This is where love really requires action. We can easily fool each other about our love for God. The fact is only you and God know the truth about that relationship. However, when it comes to the "loving others" part, the "others" will know the truth. This is where the second part of the great commandment comes in.

We need to keep in mind as we discuss LOVING OTHERS, our hearts cannot be divided. If we truly love the people in our lives then anger, resentment, bitterness and any other sinful attitude cannot exist.

READ Matthew 22:37-40

What do we learn about how we should love our neighbor?

_____

Who is our neighbor?

_____

If I don't put my love into action with others, this indicates I do not love them or God. The area we want to focus on right now is our relationship and the Love we have for our spouse. You may not be married or you may have been married once and you think this has nothing to do with you. If you are dating or thinking about dating this is for you. If you are choosing to live the rest of your life single, this is still for you because it will begin to show you how to truly love the other people in your life.

READ 1 Corinthians 13

Now we begin to see true LOVE and learn that it really is an ACTION and NOT a FEELING or an EMOTION. So, if you are ready to see your life and those around you change, let's dig in!

READ 1CORINTHIANS 13:1-3

What is Paul telling us?

_____

Keep in mind Paul is writing to other Christians. These fellow believers looked up to him and saw him as successful in the faith. What Paul is saying, in terms I can understand, is this... Let's use some of us as examples. If I could earn millions of dollars and give my family anything they asked for whenever they asked. If I don't do it in love, it means nothing. If I could solve any situation in my home or on my job, even if I do, if I do it without love, it means nothing. If I could give to the poor and tithe more than anyone could or if I could keep the nursery, drive the church bus, or teach the largest SS class, even if I could preach with the greatest, if I do it without love it means nothing.

READ 1 Corinthians 13:4
What does this say about love?

_____

The first thing we see is love suffers long. What do you think this means?

_____

_____

Some versions of the Bible use the words "love is patient". A friend of mine once explained patience to me like this. If I am in a hurry at a fast food restaurant, the cashier is taking their sweet time and talking to other employees, and I bite my tongue and smile, this is NOT long-suffering. This is patience and kindness but NOT the same thing Paul is talking about here. Remember what God does for you? (Read Psalms 103:8-10)

Paul is referring to; when someone has wronged me or attacked me and I keep my peace and deal with the situation in a Christ like manner....."Seventy times seven" (Matthew 18:22).

You do not attack or become defensive or begin to speak in a degrading manner about your attacker. You deal with it as scripture has dictated. (Read Matthew 18:15-17)

Now, how in the world does this apply to my spouse?

First, you should never speak about your spouse in a negative manner to other family members or friends. **_NEVER_** speak negatively about your spouse or your relationship to any member of the opposite sex, unless it is to your pastor, counselor, or your parents, and even then there should be great caution.

Second, you should NEVER fire back, become defensive, or belligerent. Remember, Paul tells us to suffer long.

Let's just think about this. What if we served a God who did not suffer long? What if every time we got mad at Him or committed a sin He lashed out at us?

Read Jeremiah 15:15
Who did Jeremiah count on to settle the score?

_____

It is not our place to settle the score. It is our job to resolve the conflicts in our marriages and in our relationships. If we have taken every step possible to do so and nothing is settled, then we must leave it to God and He will settle it all. But we need to make sure we have done EVERYTHING He says do.

READ 1Corinthians 13:4 again

What is the next thing we see that defines love?

We just saw that love suffers long and now we see that it is followed by "and is kind" notice here that not only do we have to suffer long, but we also have to be kind. This means that when you are under attack your only response is to be loving and kind. My wife and I have had ample opportunity to attempt to put this into practice. However, I must unfortunately report we have not always been successful, and have many times chosen not to be kind to each other. When I have done some of the utterly stupid things I have done and caused my wife great pain, she has expressed her disappointment both with and in me. She has explained my actions were like that of a child, not thinking ahead to the inevitable consequences. In that moment, I became very defensive and was quickly able to count all her wrongs. My actions in that moment were anything but Godly. According to Him, in that very moment is my chance to show her love by being long-suffering and kind. In other words, when she is sharing with me, I have two choices: I can choose an attitude of bitterness or I can choose to actually DO (action) an act of kindness. I could go fill her car up with gas or bring her a cup of tea; something that would cause her to associate my actions with love (her love language is gifts and acts of service, so this works well). People, especially women, do not want to just hear "I love you" they want to see it. This goes for all of our relationships. I can coil up like a cornered snake and strike or I can humble myself and do acts of kindness.

Let's look one more time at 1Corinthians 13:4 and see what Paul says next.

LOVE envy's not.

What does this mean?

_____

If you dissect the word ENVY in the Greek language, it means to "boil hot for". LOVE never allows such a jealousy that we would have a deep enough desire to have something that does not belong to us. Remember, back during the study of the Ten Commandments, we learned "we shall not covet"? If I have LOVE, I will not look upon another person or thing that is not mine, especially not with a burning desire to have them. This is especially true and applicable when it comes to lust. If I am living a life filled with LOVE then I won't lust after another person.

Remember, LOVE is an ACTION. I have to "do" it, I can't just say it. I have to choose to do acts of kindness; I can't choose to be envious of what belongs to someone else. You may try to justify looking at a single person lustfully thinking they don't belong to anyone. However, remember, they belong to God.

A person who is envious cannot rejoice in the success of others. Do you find yourself resenting others when God is using them? Are you envious when the neighbors have the new car, they have a new job, or they bought the big new house?
If so, then you have a sin issue and it is envy.

Notes:

DAY 2

Let's read 1Corinthians 13 again.
Read each verse slowly and dwell on every aspect of LOVE.
Begin asking yourself the question..."Do I or do I not LOVE? Does the love I practice consist of action?

Look at verse 4.
LOVE does not brag,
Write a brief interpretation of this.

"Does not brag", means I do not put myself above others. This means I must be humble, not a doormat, but my wife should be more important to me than my own desires. As the husband, according to the Bible, I am the head of the house, but her needs should be more important than mine should. I must not elevate myself above her or God. This is critical in our relationship with God. Once we begin to think our abilities or spirituality is because of something we have done, disaster is just ahead. Trust me on this one; I speak from personal experience.

In 1998 God was calling me into full time ministry in the area of counseling. I chose to back away from God and stop spending time with Him. My feelings were that if He was calling me into the ministry I must of arrived spiritually. I began to place myself on the same level with God. When you begin to think this way, your fall is not far off in the future. You will fall and trust me, the higher you put yourself on a pedestal...the farther and harder your fall becomes. I can tell you, my fall was so hard I personally felt as though I had fallen out of the sky. I know I didn't fall from heaven to earth, but it certainly felt that drastic. I had placed myself in both my mind and my heart on a level I felt was actually the same as God.

The attitude I just described is bragging. If you find yourself beginning to think that because of your knowledge, abilities, or strength that you are actually better than God is, you have just sinned against God and man. God wants us to be humble.
READ James 4:10

What does this say about God and our attitude towards Him?

_____

Also, many of you have heard this before; however, it is worth repeating. God took a rib from Adam for a reason. He took the rib to show where the wife's position should be in the relationship to her husband. It is not under his foot, or over his head but right beside him.

Now, Read 1Corinthians 13:4 once more and let's get this one last nugget out.
Write a brief description of your interpretation of "not puffed up".

_____

Not puffed up; to make haughty. LOVE is not prideful.
What is pride?
_____

The type of pride Paul is discussing here is, as Webster's Dictionary defines it, "an unduly high opinion of oneself, or arrogance". This is not saying we shouldn't take pride in a task we do and do well. However, it is speaking of having an opinion of ourselves that causes us to think better of ourselves than our spouse, our family members, our coworkers, and our church family. The focus of bragging is to build ourselves up. We can't build up two people at the same time. I am either going to build up you, or myself. If I am building myself up then I must tear you down a little. True love says "you are better than me".

What is the MAIN characteristic we have learned about LOVE so far in this Chapter?

_____

The bottom line here is we MUST be humble! We shouldn't think of ourselves as pond scum, but our Father and His children should be ahead of us. Remember the second greatest commandment? It says to love your neighbor as yourself. If you love someone as much as you love yourself, his or her needs should have the same level of urgency as yours. Their desires become your desires and their interests become your interests (assuming these are godly).

Take some time now to reflect on verse 4.
Make a list below of some of the things you could and should change to show love. Place the name of the person and the actions that need to be directed toward that person in the second column. First and foremost should be our spouse, however, don't forget your Heavenly Father and His children.

_____

_____

_____

_____

Notes:

DAY 3

Let's begin today by reviewing the first 4 verses in 1Corinthians 13.
Write out below a brief synopsis of what these 4 verses have taught us.

_____

_____

_____

_____

Also list any ACTION you have taken since reading the verses to show your love.
REMEMBER, LOVE IS A VERB AND A VERB REQUIRES ACTION!

_____

_____

_____

Read 1Corinthians 13:5
Write below your interpretation of this verse.

_____

_____

....Love is not rude
Agape Love says I care about what you want. It doesn't tune people out but instead listens intently. This love cares about what the person you are trying to Love cares about and what their dreams are.

I don't care about polished fingernails with designs, or iPod games about making food, or about clothes shopping but I have girls and a wife who do. Love says; I am willing to spend the time, I am going to care about your story….I am going to Agape you!

Not acting rudely says; your happiness matters to me!

The Greek word here means; shapeless or unformed. It has no discipline…is your Love disciplined?

…Love seeks not its own

In your own words define seek.

_____

In Luke 19:10 Jesus said He came to seek. This is the same word used in 1Corinthians 13:5. We need to be seeking others the same way Christ sought us. You are on His mind, you are who He came for, and you are the one He died for….YOU, YOU, YOU. You have been sought after already now go seek your wife, your kids, your parents and the other people God has placed in your life.

1 Corinthians 10:24… whose well-being?

_____

Now before we go further someone's name just came to your mind….maybe more than one.
Now write that name or those names.

_____

Romans 12:10, Philippians 2:14

….Love is not provoked
Agape Love does not have sudden outburst of anger. It is not looking for a fight when it has been wronged.
The word Paul uses here from the Greek means; to make angry, to burn with anger. It also means; to make sharp.

How many times have you used sharp words and then things really got worse?

Proverbs 15:1 a gentle answer turns away wrath, but a harsh word stirs up anger.

If we are going to Love the people in our lives we have to be soft and gentle not harsh in our speech and actions.

….Love thinks no evil
This means: Love does not continually keep track of and store up wrongs committed against you. Love will NEVER hold onto these!
The word used "logizomai" in the original language means to keep a record of, to calculate.
We should never keep records of wrong. God doesn't hold our past sins against us and neither should we hold others failures against them.

Psalms 103:12 How far are they away from us?

_____

The same word is used in Philippians 4:8; what things are we supposed to calculate or think about?

_____

_____

_____

Pray now for the person(s) you listed on the previous page. Also pray and ask God to help you not recount others wrongs. Ask him to help you live Philippians 4:8.

If we think bad we will feel bad, if we think evil we will act evil…change that thinking!

Read 1 Corinthians 13:1-6

I am sure you have seen the Movie Forest Gump. We were all rooting for Forest to RUN, for Forest to win and for Forest to get the girl and when he and Jenny got together, I was happy. However, I realized I was actually rooting for Forest to have an immoral relationship with Jenny.

God says not to "rejoice in unrighteousness". WOW! That hurts. I can justify rooting for Forest though because it is just a movie, right?

How many times have you and I hoped that someone would fail, or not do as good as we do, so we would look better? How many times have we celebrated in someone else's sin? How many times have we provoked someone to sin then threw it back at them. All of these are examples of "rejoicing in unrighteousness".

Romans 12:9; write this verse using your own words:

_____

_____

Love doesn't laugh or gossip about someone else's faults. Ephesians 4:29

....Love rejoices in truth
What is truth?

_____

Read John 14:6
Any great and loving relationship has to be centered on Jesus. If you want to Love those in your life make sure you are always centering things on Him. The Truth!

Love is always truthful to those they love. If you're lying (even what you think is a little lie) you do not love.

In the marriage relationship it is all too common for one spouse to ask other what's wrong and get an answer of "nothing". This is not being truthful. Don't avoid truth and say its love. If something is bothering you share it in love. (Ephesians 4:14-15).

Love that is rejoicing does so exceedingly. Exceedingly means: to an UNUSUALLY high degree. In other words, "Out of the norm".
Does this describe you?
Does your Love look out of the norm in comparison with the worlds?
Does it look like something from the television show "The Jersey Shore" or is it a picture of Jesus?
Love celebrates, rejoices, and thrives!

Notes:

Ok let's do a little Bible drill. In each verse one word describes or gives direction about Love, list that word.

Romans 13:8　　　　　　　_____

Colossians 3:14　　　　　　_____

1 Corinthians 14:1　　　　　_____

Philippians 1:9　　　　　　 _____

Hebrews 13:1　　　　　　　_____

1 Thessalonians 3:12　　　　_____

1 Peter 4:8　　　　　　　　_____

Hebrews 10:24　　　　　　　_____

Philippians 2:2　　　　　　 _____

2 Corinthians 8:8　　　　　 _____

Think about this, if we Agape, we can't sin. Only when we focus on ourselves do we sin!

In 1 Corinthians 13:7 you will see a HUGE three-letter word. It is the word ALL. It means everything not just the easy stuff it means ALL the stuff.
God knew we could handle the easy stuff so He had Paul write "ALL" things. We need to beg God for strength to deal with ALL things. I am strong enough on my own to handle the small stuff, the easy stuff but I need the power of God to handle the big stuff.

"...bears ALL things"

This literally means to cover over, hide, to protect, or to keep secret. Love doesn't go around talking about things that will hurt the person we Love.
Those we Love will hurt us: this is a fact. The way we handle the hurt will show our Love for them.
1 Peter 4:8, Proverbs 10:12

Galatians 6:1 tells us to
"pick those up who fall; not talk about them or hurt them."

"...believes ALL things"
Love sees the wrong, but believes the best.
I have a tendency at times to doubt every word that comes out of my teenager's mouth. I really struggle with believing them sometimes. I am not sure if this comes from being a teenager once and the sinful life I myself led, or if it is a lack of Love for them.
But this is what I do know...Love says; I believe ALL things until proven different by wrong actions. Love looks for the good, the positive, and the best; it does not always think the worst.

This is difficult, especially if we have been "lied to" repeatedly. If this is the case then we need to TRUST but VERIFY. This is a slow process but it is necessary to live a life of holiness before God and to love others.

If by chance you are the one who has broken trust, it can only be restored with true love, consistency, and time.

"....hopes ALL things"
Love says "failure is not final".
Failures will happen but Love says I refuse to let that define the person I am supposed to be Loving.
Is anything too hard for God? Read Isaiah 45:1-7

Luke 15:11-22 God CAN repair relationships. We have to trust Him and continue to Love. Notice how the father received him in v20. Also notice the father had HOPE, FAITH and TRUST the son was coming back....he was waiting for him!

"...endures ALL things"

This is the toughest I think. This says we "keep on keeping on". This was one of my dad's favorite sayings. It never meant much to me as a kid. As I got older I began to understand it more. It is difficult to remain / endure when you have been hurt.

But Love says I will endure!

Here is Strong's definition of the word:
1) To remain
a) To tarry behind
2) To remain i.e. abide, not recede or flee
a) To preserve: under misfortunes and trials to hold fast to one's faith in Christ
b) To endure, bear bravely and calmly: ill treatments

It can seem impossible to endure when you have been hurt badly but when we do, that is LOVE. Notice it says to bear bravely. This is something only God can do for us. He is the only one who can help us when we have experienced the worst of the worst. Notice it also says calmly. Calmness in the middle of hurt is hard but it can be a relationship changer. Proverbs 15:1

Notes:

Week 6

Day 1

"….Love never fails."

We will look at the beginning of I Corinthians 13:8 here. Paul is dealing with the Corinthian Church regarding gifts versus Love. He said Love never fails. Paul says gifts, as important as they are, will cease but Love will never cease.

Why does Love fail?

_____

_____

Remember, if it failed it wouldn't be Agape. All other forms of love can fail. The feeling of love can fail but Agape Love cannot fail.

Based on what you have learned why can't Agape fail?

_____

_____

_____

Agape can't fail because it acts. If your Love is not acting then it is not Agape. Therefore, Agape can't fail.

If you feel like love is failing in your life then your actions have failed or become sluggish. You can't wait on good feelings to cause you to love but negative feelings should cause you to go all out and ACT! Agape love is NOT an emotion but if your emotions are low then love those God has placed in your life. This will eventually cause the right emotions. Love God, Love others.

We need to make sure we are "Doing Love" (actions) with those God has placed in our lives and not people we choose to put in our lives to meet an emotional need.

In counseling I run across a lot of people who **FEEL** a certain way. Most negative feelings we have are because we are self-focused. If you want your emotions to improve, act first.

I have heard this more times than I care to count in my counseling career; "I don't feel in love anymore".

This, in most cases, is a very true statement. The problem is we have failed to grasp how God wants us to do things:

Agape (Love) the Lord
Agape (Love) others

Here is how our heart and mind typically function.

We THINK ---> We FEEL ---> We ACT ….then we repeat.

What God tells us is if we want to FEEL good and we want the people in our lives to FEEL complete, we must love (ACT) them first.

We were created to Agape God and others. We were not created to Agape ourselves this happened through sin.

Feelings will fail, but Agape never does!

There are four different words in the Greek language that are all translated into the same one word in English; LOVE. One of those Greek words is Eros. It makes sense that is where we get the English word Erotic. This type of love is based on attraction, feelings, emotions, and can be a very selfish (what it does for me) kind of love. Eros love is what causes us to want to date that certain someone. However, this love alone will never last. A portion of the love we have for our spouse will be Eros. However, a marriage based on Eros love alone will never allow us to walk through the valleys of life remaining together or be a "to death do us part" kind of love because it is based on feelings. When the negative feelings happen, and they will, we will have a battle that our own selfishness will win every time.

Paul goes on in the rest of v8-10 and explains the things THE PEOPLE hold as important are not going to last. He says when Jesus comes back all these "things" will be gone, but Agape never will. We could and should apply this to our lives.

What are you holding on to that someday will not matter?

_____

Now answer this honestly, does that thing, or relationship, hinder you from Loving God and others?

_____

If so, then you have to ask God to forgive you for the idol you have placed in your life. Then turn away from the idol and turn to God. You must remove the idol. (true repentance requires both)

Day 2

When children are small they act in ways that simply would not be acceptable for an adult.

My wife and I recently gave our youngest daughter a stuffed monkey. She named the monkey right away. She talks to the monkey. She sleeps with the monkey. She even had Roscoe's, that's the monkey's name, arm wrapped in a sling the other day because he fell and hurt his arm. She is a child; it's not strange for her to act this way. However, you would commit me to an institution if I started walking around with a stuffed monkey and was attempting to communicate with said monkey. I'm a grown man.

Paul tells the Corinthians, in a nice way….grow up!
He says; you are acting like a child, you understand like a child, and you are thinking like a child.
He says it is time to put away childish things.
As adults we don't carry around a stuffed animal and play games with it. We did that when we were children.
We need to Agape like adults, like the mature people we are. It is time to stop sitting around and whining about how we FEEL and get to work loving those around us.
This was a turning point for me in all my relationships. I used to live my life focused solely on my wants and desires. In the process I constantly sinned against God and hurt a lot of people…a lot of people.

When I began to understand Love it was life changing for me. But when I got to this verse it was a wakeup call. It was saying to me…time to **MAN UP**. Quit living like a child! You have responsibilities and relationships that need you to be the man you are supposed to be.
I think Beth Moore once said, "Stop whining and put your big girl panties on". Well, I don't have any of those but I do have some "big boy undies".

In verse 13 Paul tells us three things to abide in; faith, hope and Love

We have to have faith. We first have to have faith that Jesus is God's son and that He has risen from the dead to save our souls (Romans 10:9-10).

We also need hope. Our hope does not believe "it might be true" about Jesus coming again but a confident expectation that He is coming back. Living and loving our lives as if we believe it is going to happen.

Then he says the greatest of these is Love.
It is the greatest because love is who God is. God is love. He loved us so much He gave...Will you?

Notes:

Day 3

Why is Love so tough?

Love is tough because we are "fallen" people loving other "fallen" people. People can make Love hard because of the way they treat us. Paul didn't say we get a pass just because someone is difficult to love.

A common phrase I hear when counseling is "you just don't know how they have treated me", "you just don't know what they said about me". God didn't call us to a life of easy. He called us to a life of holy; a life that loves the unlovable. Sometimes we will be treated in ways we don't like. Sometimes people will say things that hurt us but that never excuses us from loving them.

I heard a country song not long ago "If I could have a beer with Jesus". At my first listen I was shocked, but out of curiosity I continued listening to the song. Then the lyrics "how did you turn the other cheek to save a sorry soul like me" played. If we could comprehend what it took for Jesus to save us, then loving others wouldn't be so hard. See this guy (Thomas Rhett Akins) in the song understood it took turning the other cheek to Love like God calls us to Love.

What if God had never turned the other cheek when I slapped Him in the face….over and over and over?

Do you remember what we said earlier about a heart divided? Our hearts cannot multi-task. We will Love or we will not love but we can't do both.

Read Matthew 6:24. What does it say about serving two masters?

You can't do both. But notice it says he will HATE the one and LOVE the other.

This is true in our relationships as well. Hate sounds like a very harsh opposite to Love, that's because it is. But it is the opposite of Agape. Both are verbs and both require action. If we are not acting one way then we must be acting the other.

Not only does being hurt by someone make it difficult to Love but also unforgiveness makes it impossible to Love. If we harbor unforgiveness it is the same thing as hate. Jesus told us to forgive so we could be forgiven. Read Matthew 6:12-14, Jesus said we were supposed to come to the Father asking Him to forgive our debts AS we were forgiving those indebted to us. He didn't say for me to ask for forgiveness and *then* give it. He said to ask Him to forgive me AS I AM Forgiving others. I need to be forgiving if I want to be forgiven. *Forgiveness is also a verb*. But the idea is we will live in an attitude of forgiveness.

Love and unforgiveness cannot reside in the same heart! Read Colossians 3:1-15 List the things Paul says to do away with and then list the things he said to do as a new man. Pay close attention to verse 13 (forgiveness) and pay close attention to verse 14. What makes perfect harmony?

Notes:

Day 4

Read Colossians 3:1-15 again

What has Love got to do with it?

In Tina Turner's song "What's love got to do with it" she says that love is a second hand emotion. This is many times the case because people are waiting on a good feeling to happen before they act. Paul says it is not the feeling but the action that brings harmony to relationships.

Harmony, it is a beautiful thing. When you hear groups sing a beautiful song and then they begin to harmonize it is awesome!

In this passage Paul states that Love "binds in harmony". So, if we want harmony in our relationships, we must have agape love for each other.

Agape has No divisions. It works together and causes things to run smoothly.

Many married couples say we just don't like being around each other. We are cold to each other. We fight all the time. Why? *There is no Love.* God says where there is Love there will be unity and harmony.

Agape is NOT a feeling nor is it an emotion.

It is so important: Jesus said it sums up the whole Law, all 613 commands in the Law.

Wow, one word, one thing…..just Agape! That's powerful!

You will never reach harmony, unity, or peace, for that matter, chasing after your own ideas of Love. It only happens when you chase after (serve, act) God and your neighbor. By the way, neighbor equals all human life; family, friend, and foe.

Notes:

Mind, Feelings & Actions

The mind is where all of our choices and decisions begin. Our minds are where we decide if we will follow God or follow ourselves.

Read Romans 12:1-2

What does it say we have to do to be different from the world?

_____

The world's view of love is completely based on feelings. If it feels good "do it" is the world's view and sadly many Christians agree. However, Gods love is not based on feelings, but instead based on TRUTH. The amazing thing is if you follow Gods agape love based on truth you ultimately will arrive at the feeling. But Gods love requires action and obedience and then the feeling comes not always immediately but eventually.

If agape Love were really taking place in the world and in the church (the body of Christ) the divorce rate would be at 0. However, this is obviously not the case and the reason is because we are searching for a self-fulfilling emotion instead of being willing to do a self-sacrificing act.

This sinful pattern begins when we allow our minds to focus on our needs and desires. This is why God says don't act like this world but renew your mind so you can be transformed.

We need to be transformed into little Christ's. Men and women who are more concerned about doing what God asks us to do than what we feel like doing. Imagine if Christ had not been obedient to the Father and said "I don't feel like Loving and Sacrificing for these people". Instead, He was obedient to the Father and full of love for us and we must act like Him. We need to transform our minds through His word.

Many of the couples I see for marriage counseling often amaze me, keep in mind the majority of my clients are professing Christians. Usually, as a marriage counselor you are a couple's last resort before heading to divorce attorneys. However, I have had more than one couple walk in with divorce papers in hand saying "Unless you can do something to fix this quick, we're going to file these". In a few cases that last sentence ended with the words "tomorrow". Couples spend years ruining and tearing apart their marriage, however, they want it all put back together in perfect condition in one day.

I always begin by asking the same questions.
Have you come to a place in your life where you have allowed Jesus to become your Savior and Lord?
I usually hear a testimony of salvation but I have had the honor of leading many people to the Lord for the first time at this point. Sometimes they have professed a faith but they truly had never committed their lives to Him.

The responses I receive to the next question always baffles me:

On a scale of 1 to 10, with 10 being the best, tell me how you would rate your relationship with God, I have never had anyone who will say they are less than 4; most people say 5-7. Let that sink in for a moment. I have people sitting in front of me ready to divorce, some who have had affairs and some who "just fell out of love", telling me their relationship with God is average or above????

Some people really believe they can be in right relationship with God while simultaneously being out of harmony, unity, or Love with the person they are married to "for better or for worse".

I have had people tell me, "I don't have a problem with God; I have a problem with him/her".

God says if we have a problem with him/her we have a problem with Him.

Read Matthew 5:21-24 what does it say do if there is a problem? What does it say we must do?

_____

God wants our relationships to be right first before we come to Him. If we are out of sorts in our earthly relationships we are out of sorts with Him.

But in our minds we seem to somehow justify our actions. In our minds we have all the reasons why it's okay not to Love someone. In our minds we have allowed thoughts to transform into hate, bitterness, anger, rage and all kinds of malice. In our minds we have allowed Satan to get a foothold.

It is in our minds that we have lost the will or desire to Love our neighbor. It is in our minds where we must begin to fight the battle and win against Satan.

In Philippians 4:8 the Bible tells us eight things to think about continually. List them below.

_____

_____

_____

_____

_____

_____

_____

_____

We will need to transform our minds through His word. We will need to think on the things of Him. And we must ACT.

A proper action will get you the feeling you are looking for and a proper thought life will help you keep it.

You can't think your way into Agape. You have to ACT!

It sometimes may seem insurmountable but the God of the universe is waiting to help you!

Read Jeremiah 29:11
God is with you!

During this past 6 weeks you have discovered the truth about love and ways to begin putting it into action. My hope is you will begin to act today. Remember I wrote this Bible Study from my own personal journey and I know how hard it is to take the next step. I know that doing things the way God asks us to is not at all easy sometimes. However, this is what I can tell you; He took every step with me. He increased my strength on every step I committed to make. He helped me deal with my prideful heart and through love crushed my selfish desires. The more I loved others the less I loved myself. The more I poured out, the more He poured in. I found the feelings I was looking for but not by the same methods I had tried for the majority of my life. I found them by Loving Him and Loving Them.

I would like to thank my wonderful wife for all the work she did in helping me write this study.

God bless you baby!

Made in the USA
Columbia, SC
16 June 2017